In the first senten[ces] ... Bolton explains [that ... comedy is ...] to be funny. Its purpos[e] ... and [is not] an argument. It's not to prove that your political beliefs are more sophisticated than those who hold a different opinion. It's not an excuse to use language that people may feel uncomfortable listening to. Humor's purpose is to make people laugh and enjoy. My colleague, Martha Bolton, was always able to uncover that humor, mine it, polish it, and get laughs with it. This book is a great indication of that skill. If you want examples of good, solid, funny comedy, read Martha's new book, *Forgettable Jokes for Older Folks*. It's chock-full of them.

—Gene Perret, three-time Emmy Award winning comedy writer for Bob Hope, *The Carol Burnett Show*, and *Mama's Family*, and author of over forty books

I would love to go inside Martha Bolton's brain, but I might get knocked over by all the funny ideas zooming around in there. Martha has written for a host of comedians, including me—going all the way back to when we were both young, had a lot more energy, and no gray hairs to cover up. We're older now and a lot has changed. Thank God our friendship isn't one of them.

—Mark Lowry, recording artist, "Mary, Did You Know" lyricist

Martha Bolton can take any topic and turn it into comedy gold. The quantity that she can produce is unmeasurable. The quality she creates is unbelievable.

—Earl Musick, cartoonist, comedian, and speaker

Martha Bolton is a powerhouse joke writer. Her ability to take a single topic and drill down into it for the comedy gold is amazing. It's like watching a root canal on current events! When you add Martha to an idea, you get loads of funny! She's got a gift, she's honed it, and we are all the better for it.

—Rik Roberts, comedian and CEO of School for Laughs

The Bible tells us in Proverbs 7:22 that "A merry heart doeth good like a medicine." Well, lucky for you, our great friend "doctor Martha" has just penned you a priceless 192-page prescription. Be a good patient: read it and get well soon.

—Derrick Tennant, comedian, 14 Sleeves

Forgettable Jokes for Older Folks

Jokes You Wish You Could
Remember about Things You
Thought You'd Never Forget

BY

MARTHA BOLTON

BroadStreet
PUBLISHING

BroadStreet Publishing® Group, LLC
Savage, Minnesota, USA
BroadStreetPublishing.com

Forgettable Jokes for Older Folks: Jokes You Wish You Could
Remember about Things You Thought You'd Never Forget

978-1-4245-5777-6 (softcover)
978-1-4245-5778-3 (e-book)

Stock or custom editions of BroadStreet Publishing titles
may be purchased in bulk for educational, business, ministry,
fundraising, or sales promotional use. For information, please
email info@broadstreetpublishing.com.

Cover design by Chris Garborg at garborgdesign.com
Typesetting by Kjell Garborg at garborgdesign.com

Printed in the United States of America
18 19 20 21 22 5 4 3 2 1

To the person, whose name escapes me,
for their unforgettable words,
which I also can't seem to recall right now.
But whatever they were,
and whoever said them,
they were the inspiration behind this book.

What's Funny?

Have you ever wondered what happened to the days when comedy was just plain funny? It wasn't mean-spirited, even if it was a "roast." Respect was the undertone of the ribbing, and usually the evening was capped off with a genuine tribute. The Dean Martin roasts, the Friars Club roasts, and even Don Rickles would stick to good-natured insults. And it was funny. So much so that even the subject of the jokes would laugh along with everyone else.

What passes for "roasting" today, however, is too often little more than a barrage of mean-spirited, agenda-driven "jokes," without filter or tact. They seem to forget that roasts are reserved for people who are admired, loved, and respected. Otherwise, the "roast" becomes uncomfortable for everyone— the audience and the people on the dais. The guest of honor is unfairly berated and perhaps even responds in kind. The whole affair can do comedy a disservice. And too often it ends up on the evening news.

Remember the days when comedy was neither mean-spirited, nor agenda-driven? It was fun to listen, to laugh, and to tear up during the final tribute. Even political satirists were even-handed when dishing out their humor. Comedians like Bob Hope, Johnny Carson, Mark Russell, and going all the way back to Will Rogers and Mark Twain were not motivated by their personal opinions. Their goal was simply to make their audiences laugh. Republicans, Democrats, Independents—it didn't matter. The comics were equal opportunity jokesters. People of all political leanings would likely be in their audience, and they joked about them all.

Remember the days when marital humor was covered by the likes of Lucille Ball, Jackie Gleason, George Burns, Gracie Allen, and so many other talents? Regardless of what they said, their humor was grounded in love, tolerance, and respect.

For family life humor, we had Dick Van Dyke and Mary Tyler Moore, Danny Thomas, Ozzie and Harriet, *The Brady Bunch*, or we could just *Leave it to Beaver*. Later, there was *Sanford and Son, Everybody Loves Raymond, Family Matters*, and so many others. Even *The Addams Family* and *The Munsters* gave families plenty to laugh about.

For the foibles of life there was Bob Newhart, Rodney Dangerfield, Milton Berle, Sid Caesar, and a host of others who could make us guffaw at the drop of a punchline. For pure zaniness, there was Jerry Lewis, Phyllis Diller, Jonathan Winters, and Robin Williams. Domestic complaints? Joan Rivers. Senior life and friendship? *The Golden Girls*. Small town? Andy Griffith and Don Knotts.

Some comics didn't need words to make us laugh. Talents such as Red Skelton or Harpo Marx proved that. Some delivered their comedy through other means, like ventriloquist Edgar Bergen and his sidekick, Charlie McCarthy.

There are far too many talented comedians and comic actors of yesteryear to list them all here, but in my opinion, they all had one thing in common. Their comedy was the kind that made you feel good afterwards. You thought about your own problems a little less. You laughed along with people of opposing political beliefs and different life experiences, and it didn't matter. Not one iota. Barriers were dropped, not erected. Hearts were opened a little, not slammed shut.

I miss those comedians and television shows.

Some of today's comics do understand the gift those legendary talents gave us, and they try to replicate that brand of comedy. They know that life is tough for everybody and that humor is powerful and a necessity in life, medicinal even, so they use it conscientiously. They realize we all *want* to laugh. We all *need* to laugh—especially these days. They understand a comic's job isn't to create more pain for anyone. Humor's most noble and greatest mission is simply this: to make us *all* laugh. Preferably together.

Martha Bolton

IT'S NOT OVER YET

KEEPING UP APPEARANCES

Facial and Bodily Changes, Fashion Tips, and More

I'm comfortable in my own skin. Why shouldn't I be? It's not that tight of a fit.

• • •

I wear a size 12, but my skin's a size 14. It's like one too many people told me to hang loose.

• • •

When they talk about getting your swag on, I don't think this is what they meant.

• • •

Do you know what it's like to roll up your sleeves and realize you're not wearing any?

. . .

Some days I look in the mirror and think I'm growing my own turtleneck.

. . .

My mother had a neck like this. I had no idea it was contagious.

. . .

Wrinkles? My face has seen more lines than the unemployment office.

. . .

They say wrinkles tell a story. If that's true, my forehead is a mini-series.

. . .

I'd wear bangs, but I have a hard-enough time keeping my forehead out of my eyes.

. . .

It's a bad day when you reach up to take your sun visor off only to realize it was just your eyelids dropping into your line of vision.

. . .

My eyebrows are drooping down so low in front of my eyes—I can pluck them without using a mirror.

. . .

I believe gravity has gained weight.
Just ask yourself: Is it harder for
you to get up from a sitting position
these days? More difficult for you
to climb out of bed in the morning?
Do you find you can hardly hold
your head and shoulders upright?
It isn't you. It's gravity. It keeps
gaining weight, and we just can't
keep lifting it up anymore.

• • •

"Gravity"
(To the Tune of "Yesterday")

Gravity

Wish this wasn't how things had to be.

Body parts are falling off of me.

Oh, why did God make gravity?

Can you see

How my figure has dropped to my knees?

Not much else is where it used to be

Since I lost out to gravity.

Why can't things just stay where God put them long ago?

All day long I'm warning others to "Look out below!"

Gravity.

I've been shrinking, now I'm half of me.

I might not stop until I'm four foot three.

Oh, why did God make gravity?

• • •

Movies for Seniors

Hey, Dude, Where's My Teeth?

• • •

Legally Grey

• • •

Florida's Most Wanted

• • •

Gangs of Palm Beach

• • •

Cold Feet Manor

• • •

Near Total Recall

• • •

Man in the Iron Lung

• • •

Sleepless in Every City

• • •

Catch You If I Can

• • •

The Rock (And the Rest of My Kidney Stones)

• • •

More Facial and Bodily Changes, Fashion Tips, and More

They say wrinkles are simply the tracks left behind by your smiles … so apparently, my smiles have been playing with the Harlem Globetrotters.

• • •

I'd like to go back to the days when crow's feet were only something you worried about in an Alfred Hitchcock film.

• • •

An elderly movie star who appeared on the Bob Hope show had a good idea. She'd pull her skin back and tape it behind her ears. I tried that once, but all we had in the house at the time was duct tape and the silver showed through my bangs.

• • •

Wouldn't it be great if we could just unzip our skin, take it to the dry cleaners and let them shrink it back into shape?

• • •

I don't understand why it is that if we've already got crepey skin, shouldn't someone be throwing us a party?

• • •

And cellulite is a problem. My legs have seen more potholes than Interstate 40.

• • •

The other day a swarm of bees tried to make honey in one of my thighs.

• • •

But I finally found a way to get rid of unsightly cellulite … medieval body armor.

• • •

I don't get it. We're at the age where doctors are telling us to limit our cheese intake, and here it goes, showing up on our thighs.

• • •

And where do our waists go once we pass fifty? Is there a convention somewhere we don't know about? After all the years of catering to them, how can they just leave without saying goodbye?

• • •

They say a tan can make you look younger. So I tried a tanning bed. All I got was rest.

• • •

I even tried a spray-on tan, but I had to be pressure washed first.

• • •

These days, I tan the easy way. I just wait for my liver spots to connect.

• • •

I have so many liver spots, I should come with a side of onions.

. . .

Liver spots: A tan on the installment plan.

. . .

And I know I've got bags under my eyes. But Southwest lets you bring two on board for free.

. . .

And have you noticed that after a certain age, your toenails start growing to incredible lengths? There's actually an advantage to this. Now you can go swimming and spearfishing at the same time.

. . .

And think of all the rototilling jobs you could take care of by just walking barefoot through your yard.

. . .

And remember Howard Hughes? I still don't understand why he let his fingernails and toenails grow so long. Didn't he have enough whisks around the house?

• • •

I can understand the convenience of growing your own can opener at the tip of your fingers, but that really is a bit eccentric, isn't it?

• • •

In our senior years, our feet go through a lot of changes. My arches, like the Roman Empire, have long since fallen.

• • •

My secret to staying young is good food, plenty of exercise, and a make-up man with a spray gun.

• • •

I have a wonderful make-up crew. They're the same people restoring the Statue of Liberty.

• • •

Hollywood and New York fashion designers give us an unrealistic idea of what we're supposed to look like, don't they? I haven't seen a movie star with baggy skin since E.T.

• • •

The Look of Films to Come

Instead of aging gracefully, too many actors these days are opting for repeated Botox injections and, unfortunately, some are losing all natural facial expression. It's gotten so bad that producers have a new dilemma on their hands … emotionless actors.

So, screenwriters and playwrights have had to adapt. Here is a scene from one of my scripts that will demonstrate what I mean:

On the Veranda (Evening)

Charley takes Roxanne into his arms.

CHARLEY: Oh, Roxanne, I've missed you so much.

Roxanne looks into Charley's wide-open eyes. They seem open a little too wide and are somewhat alarming under the moonlight. She smiles … we think.

ROXANNE: I've missed you too, Charley.

Charley pulls Roxanne closer to him. She puckers her lips, but nothing moves.

CHARLEY: What's wrong, Roxanne?

Roxanne hesitates, wondering if her lips are still there. Charley furrows his brow … at least he would, if he could.

ROXANNE: Oh, Charley. It's just that … it's just that … you didn't call me last night.

CHARLEY: I wanted to, Sweetheart, but my cell phone died.

Roxanne turns away. She appears to be frowning, but Charley is confused. It's the same look she had earlier when she was laughing. But he presses on.

CHARLEY: Marry me, Roxanne. I've always loved you.

Charley gives an "open eye" wink. Who knew that was even possible? Roxanne turns her face back toward him (at least most of it moves), and then falls into his arms.

ROXANNE: Oh, Charley. Yes, yes … I will marry you.

Charley is elated. Despite their expressionless faces (is it joy, anger, or total distain?), he believes in his heart that she truly loves him. And he loves her.

ROXANNE: Oh, Charley.

CHARLEY: Oh, Roxanne.

The two share a pucker-free kiss. And from that day forth, they live happily ever after … although who could?

• • •

Happy Birthday

I'm not saying how many candles were on my birthday cake this year, but I think we could have roasted a rotisserie chicken over it.

• • •

My husband and I don't do birthday candles anymore. The bonfires were getting too hard to control.

• • •

Birthdays come and go … but if you sign a birthday card in pencil, it can be circulated forever.

• • •

I don't understand why people lie about their age. If I had to wait for my senior discount, they should have to wait for theirs, too.

• • •

I just had my DNA tested. They referred me to the Smithsonian.

. . .

You know you're getting old when you buy Geritol by the six-pack.

. . .

I'm so old, my birth certificate fossilized two years ago.

. . .

I recently read in the newspaper that the oldest living person recently died at the age of 117. But I checked my pulse and it wasn't me, so I went ahead and got out of bed.

. . .

The lady who lived to be 117 said her secret was eating three eggs, two of which were raw, every day for ninety years. A treadmill wasn't even mentioned … nor was a salad bar. I'm just saying.

. . .

I asked a salesclerk if she could suggest something that would make my body look good on the beach this summer. She said, "Sure. Bury most of it in the sand."

• • •

Sayings for Senior T-shirts

Complain It Forward

• • •

Walk a Mile in My Shoe Inserts

• • •

I Nap for Those Who Can't

• • •

I'd Rather Be Wheezing

• • •

Don't Make Me Use My Senior Voice!

• • •

Keep Calm and Hose Down the Candles

• • •

Car Keys: So Close and Yet So Far Away

• • •

Is There Life after 7 P.M.?

• • •

My Recliner Is the Journey

• • •

Senior Definitions

Recliner: What any ancient king would have traded his kingdom for.

• • •

Senior discount: Just one more reason to wake up in the morning.

• • •

Ideal Recliner Attachments

Holder for fishing pole

• • •

Right sidearm Keurig machine

• • •

Left sidearm mini-fridge for snacks and soda

• • •

Pop up hibachi grill for hot items
hidden in leg rest

• • •

Motion detection floodlight and perimeter
barbed wire for unauthorized entry

• • •

Activation button for transforming into golf cart

• • •

• • •

Suggested Memoir Title

I Don't Owe You an Explanation,
but Here It Is Anyway

• • •

MARTHA'S COMEDY WRITING MEMORIES

A fellow Bob Hope writer received a late-night call from Bob one night. The writer's wife answered, and Bob asked her if her husband was there. Seeing him lying next to her, sound asleep already, and not wanting to wake him up yet again for another comedy writing assignment, she thought quickly and said, "No, he told me he was going to be with you tonight." There was a pause, and then Bob said, "Oh, yeah. Here he comes now."

• • •

Exercising Your Prerogative

I do twenty jumping jacks every morning.
Well, for half of those I just clap.

• • •

Today is the first day of the rest of my push-up.

• • •

Does a sit-up count if there's a recliner
involved?

• • •

I tried a treadmill … but my pillow kept getting
stuck in the conveyor belt.

• • •

According to my pedometer, I walk twenty
thousand steps every morning. And that's just
looking for my car keys. If I lose my cell phone
too, I'm going out for the Olympics.

• • •

I swim four laps a day. I'd do more, but it's not that easy turning around in a jacuzzi.

• • •

I just did fifteen minutes of strength training. I opened a bag of potato chips.

• • •

Did you know Zumba spelled backwards is "hammock"? Okay, not really … well, it might be if you use autocorrect.

• • •

Doing squats are supposed to be good for you. But do you realize there's only a two-letter difference between the words squat and splat?

• • •

What I want to know is this: Does a 26-mile marathon count if it involves a hotel stay at the halfway point?

• • •

I do twenty minutes of water aerobics every morning. Well, some people call it getting out of the bathtub.

. . .

Did you know memory cells die faster with physical exertion? They must. Think about it: How many times have you walked into a room to get something only to stand there looking around wondering why you're there?

. . .

Senior definition of *muscle tone*: The pitch of my slapping thighs during jumping jacks.

. . .

My workout uniform is a neck brace and ten yards of Ace bandages.

. . .

The other day I took my grandchildren to the park and showed them what I could do on the parallel bars ... like tie a hammock from them.

. . .

They say swimming is good for us. But once I find my golf ball, I'm ready to call it a day.

. . .

Any senior who says they don't exercise doesn't have grandchildren.

. . .

I start every day with stretches—I stretch my jeans, my shirt, my budget …

. . .

I tried a knee bend once. It's now a new pretzel shape at Annie's.

. . .

My muscles are very flexible. I can get them to sag either to the left or to the right.

. . .

Do the Math

I recently read an article in a magazine that said I could add six months to my life if I would just exercise more. So I did the math. If I run a mile every day for the rest of my life, (for the sake of this illustration, let's say thirty years), that's 10,950 miles—10,957 miles counting the leap years. Now, forget about using an eight-minute mile as a basis. It would take me closer to thirty minutes and a taxi to run that distance. That being the case, we're talking approximately 5,479 hours spent just running. That works out to roughly 228 days, which is a little more than seven months. So my total exercising time is seven months, while it only gains me six months. Are you following my logic here? I would lose seven months jogging in order to gain six months of life. That doesn't make mathematical sense, does it? I wouldn't even be enjoying those extra seven months. Sorry, but the incentive just isn't there for me … I'm not getting a big enough return on my sweat. The math just doesn't add up.

• • •

I've got body parts falling to sleep at all hours of the day and night. It just isn't fair. Why should I be getting only seven or eight hours of sleep a night while my right leg is getting twelve?

• • •

And I tend to get colder than most people. I get cold in the car, the house, lava pits …

• • •

Thou Art What Thou Snacketh Upon

Remember when they said chocolate was bad for us? Now they're saying it's rich in antioxidants and is actually good for us. Frankly, I'm not surprised. I have always known that Hershey's would look great in an IV bag.

• • •

You know it's time to get off your diet when you watch a *Rawhide* rerun and barbeque sauce comes to mind.

• • •

I've been trying to eat right. I've stocked my freezer with salmon, mahi-mahi, and orange roughy. I found they sit quite nicely on top of the Ben & Jerry's.

• • •

Carrots are my favorite vegetable. If held upright, they can carry up to five glazed donuts.

• • •

The older you get, the tougher it is to lose weight because by then your body and your fat are really good friends.

• • •

I don't like all these pesticides they're putting on our fruit. It's gotten so bad that now when you bite into an apple and find a worm, chances are it's just trying to get out.

• • •

Personally, I don't see why I need twelve grains in my bread. I'm making a sandwich, not a patio.

• • •

It used to be that you just had to worry about your cereal getting soggy. Now you have to worry about it warping.

• • •

I don't eat a lot of fish. It's just a policy of mine. I prefer not to eat those with whom I've golfed.

• • •

"The Raven-ing"

Once upon a diet dreary,
I lay famished, weak, and weary.

Hunger pangs were far too painful
for my stomach to ignore.

Bathroom scale, it was just mocking.
Still, I would have eaten caulking,

if somebody wasn't knocking,
knocking at my condo door.

"Must be Pizza Hut," I muttered,
"knocking at my condo door.
Double cheese, I'm praying for."

I was on the Atkins diet
'til a breadstick caused a riot.

On to Weight Watchers to try it,
hoping that I could eat more.

But they had a rule they followed,
a whole ham could not be swallowed.

So, in self-pity I wallowed,
scooping crumbs up off my floor.

Then I heard more of that knocking,
tapping, rapping at my door,
and wondered who it could be for.

Oh, I've dreamed of eating Twinkies,
licking filling off my pinkies.

Scrambled eggs and sausage linkies,
Little Debbie cakes galore!

Dreamed of sourdough from Frisco,
every snack sold by Nabisco,
chocolate bars and even Crisco.

Could I last a second more?
I was starved down to my core!

Drat this diet evermore!

It is water I'm retaining,
that's the reason for my gaining.

And don't think that I'm complaining,
I just need to eat some more!

I love fat, I won't deny it.
Food is better when you fry it!

See a Snickers and I buy it,
then I keep on wanting more!

Drat this diet evermore!

So, I turned the knob and then I
opened up the door, but when I
saw the one who wanted in, I
had to shut the door again.

'Twas my trainer looking for me.
"Work out now!" she would implore me.

How I wish she'd just ignore me,
but she said I must weigh in.

"Look at all that weight you've packed on!
All the burgers you have macked on!

All the Ding Dongs you have snacked on!"
She screamed all that at me and more.

With the accusations flying,
I assured her I was trying.

I was starving, maybe dying,
but she heard me out no more.

Made me promise I would diet.
Then, told me to be quiet.

Exercise? I was to try it.
So, I did what she implored.

I stepped back and took position.
I would stop her inquisition.

Did a leg lift in submission
as I kicked her out the door!

Drat this diet evermore!

Now I'm back to eating Twinkies,
licking filling off my pinkies,
scrambled eggs and sausage linkies,
Little Debbie cakes galore.

I don't need no weight loss planning.
Zumba classes I'll be banning.

In the space that I'll be spanning,
I'll be happy to my core!

And I'll be hungry nevermore!

• • •

The Five People You Meet... in a Buffet Line

If you like buffets, one thing is certain—you're sure to meet the following five people:

- **Buffet Charley**: Charley has hit every buffet east of the Mississippi, and you can tell.

  Like the state stickers my parents used to display on the windows of our station wagon informing the world where we'd been, Buffet Charley has the same idea, only he does it with gravy stains:

  See that one there? That's the sausage gravy I had down in Florida. And that one over there? That's the turkey and giblet gravy I had in Kansas. And that one right there, well, that's the country white gravy and mashed potatoes I had down in Amarillo.

- **Muumuu Mama**: Anyone who has ever been to a buffet has seen her. Muumuu Mama is serious about her buffet experience.

  The muumuu she's wearing may or may not match her house slippers, but whatever you do, don't get in her way. You are a mere mortal and no match for such speed and agility. Just as you reach for the corn bread dressing, quick as a flash she beats you to it. Reach for some steamed carrots, and she's already got her hand on the spoon. Go for the turnip greens, and she appears out of nowhere and scoops some onto her plate first. She has the reflexes of a Wild West gunfighter and the cunning of a stealth fighter pilot. She'll beat you every time. And she's the master of disguise. She may look like a size eighteen under all of that flowing material, but Muumuu Mama weighs in at less than a hundred pounds. The muumuu disguises the thirty pounds of muffins she's smuggling out for later.

- **Finger-Licking Freddie**: Watching Finger-Licking Freddie is like watching a ballet.

  As he dishes out his food, it's *The Nutcracker Meets Emeril* or *Swan Lake Meets Uncle Ben.* First, he scoops some potatoes and gravy onto his plate, then gracefully raises his hand to his mouth and samples it. Yum. Without missing a beat, he glides down the aisle and dishes up some salad. Some of the ranch dressing drips down the side of his plate, but not to worry. Finger-Licking Freddie simply slides his finger along the rim, and gracefully licks his fingers again. He makes a quarter turn and moves on to the meat station. Enjoying a drip of gravy that landed on his palm, he grabs a roll, and sneaks a taste of the freshly melted butter on top. He ladles and shovels (and samples) until by the time he makes it to the last food station, he's already consumed 1,800 calories! An audience would have erupted in applause! Every move has been the epitome of grace and style—perfectly in sync to the background music.

- **Chicken Wing Darla**: This is the lady who will eat an entire tray of chicken wings—savoring every molecule of meat, then stacking the ravaged bones onto her plate like a pile of greasy firewood.

For only having four teeth, it's quite a feat. Frankly, I try to leave a little bit of meat on my chicken bones simply out of respect. I figure if the animal laid down his life for my lunch, the least I can do is leave him a little dignity … and gristle.

- **Juggling Jimmy**: He is the easiest of the five to spot because of all the plates he juggles between food stations.

  Jimmy believes in getting his money's worth. Sometimes he'll even arrive late for lunch just so his meal will run into dinner and he won't miss any new menu options.

There you have it—the five people you meet, not in heaven, but in the buffet line. But who knows? Heaven might have the best buffet yet!

• • •

12-Step Program for Buffet Addicts

1. Admit that you are powerless over fried chicken legs and gizzard gravy.

2. Believe that a power greater than you is pulling you to the yams and cinnamon butter.

3. Surrender that third plate over to the waitress. Just because you can have "all you can eat" doesn't mean you should.

4. Take an inventory of your pockets and your handbag before exiting a restaurant. Any muffin or roll that you find should be relinquished.

5. Admit to yourself and another human being the exact number of calories you consumed during your last buffet experience. Compare it with the national budget.

6. Be ready to be intercepted by the manager on your way to the ice cream machine. It's for your own good.

7. Know your "ladle limits." The idea is not to drown your salad with the bleu cheese dressing but to simply dribble the dressing over it.

8. Make a list of any and all persons that you may have cut off in line or unintentionally offended when you snatched up the last chicken wing before they could maneuver it onto their plate. Be willing to make amends.

9. If possible, go ahead and make amends to each one of these people, unless they are bigger than you and are still ticked off.

10. Continue to make a regular assessment of your buffet weaknesses and record your successes. How do they compare?

11. Share this new knowledge with other buffet addicts, so that they too can kick the all-you-can-eat-buffet habit.

12. If you find you truly can't stop going to buffets, then go on and go … and save me a seat.

• • •

Middle Age Fashion Faux Pas

I say it's perfectly okay for a person on the north side of middle age to dress younger than their birth certificates designate. However, there do need to be some guidelines. So here is my list.

The following combinations do not go together under any circumstances:

- A nose ring and bifocals

- Spiked hair and bald spots

- A pierced tongue and dentures

- Mini-skirts and support hose

- Ankle bracelets and corn pads

- A belly button ring and a gall bladder surgery scar

• • •

Frankly, I think one of our own should be designing our swimwear. No matter how hard I try, I can never find one in my style—long sleeves and a turtleneck.

• • •

Do you have any idea how depressing it is to try on an "irregular" and it fits perfectly?

• • •

The problem with "one size fits all" is that they never tell you "all of what?" Your left leg? Your right shoulder? Your pinky finger?

• • •

Social Security, Retirement, Part Time Jobs... or Where'd All the Money Go?

Retirement is never having to beg for days off anymore … except from your wife.

• • •

Retirees spend a lot of time praying … especially at the ATM.

• • •

Comebacks for Seniors

"I don't mean to be difficult, but you make it so necessary."

• • •

"When I come back with my oxygen tank, you'll be sorry."

• • •

"Think you got in the last word? I had my hearing aid turned off."

• • •

Ten Commandments for Aging

1. Thou shalt not raise up thy pants unto the uttermost parts of thy armpits.

2. Thou shalt not look at thy face in a magnifying mirror, for thy heart's sake.

3. Thou shalt not curse the name of thy dietary plan.

4. Remember the place where thou has left thy car keys, glasses, and other possessions, or buy tracking devices.

5. Honor the rules of spandex that the circulation in thy legs may be long on this earth.

6. Thou shalt not steal the age of thy neighbor.

7. Thou shalt not commit to babysit more than six grandchildren under the age of three at one time, lest thou become a babbling loon.

8. Thou shalt wear comfortable shoes so that thou wouldst not have a harvest of bunions and corn.

9. Thou shalt not bear false witness with thy comb-over.

10. Thou shalt not covet thy neighbor's taco, hot and spicy sausage, or any other tasty morsel that thou knowest will war against the innermost regions of thy body.

• • •

On the Road Again: Driving, Flying, Cruising, RVs, and More

I was just involved in a nine-car pileup. But it's not as bad as it sounds. It was at four different intersections.

• • •

I have a full-time police escort. Unfortunately, he's always behind me.

• • •

I have a bumper sticker that says, "I brake on impact."

• • •

I've been in bumper-to-bumper traffic all day. It wasn't congested. That's just how I drive.

• • •

An Open Letter to Drivers Who Tailgate Us

Dear Driver Who Won't Back Off Our Bumper,

It has come to our attention—by looking in our rearview mirror—that we are apparently not driving fast enough for you. We apologize for this oversight on our part. We saw a sign a few miles back that stated the speed limit was forty-five miles per hour. But because you are going an estimated seventy miles per hour, we must be mistaken. We were not aware that seventy is the new forty-five.

We can tell by the look on your face that our slowness is bothering you. You might even think that we are doing it intentionally just to tick you off. We assure you this is not the case. Sitting too long at an intersection after the light has turned green is what we do to intentionally tick you off, not driving slowly.

Please feel free to go ahead and pass us if you like, but kindly refrain from honking your horn as you do so. We are not used to sudden loud noises coming from behind us. (We know what you're thinking, but that's not what we meant.)

Should you refuse to share the road with us in a more respectful and less aggressive way, we will be forced to do the only thing we can do—brake for absolutely no reason at all. We don't want to be introduced to you this way, but your actions will leave us no choice.

Thank you for your consideration to our request.

Sincerely,

Senior Drivers of America

• • •

It Might Be Time to Give up Your Driver's License If ...

You've ever waited at an intersection through three or more light changes before making your left turn.

• • •

You consider the median your personal driving lane.

• • •

You've ever worn out a new brake light on a two-mile trip to the store.

• • •

You've ever honked at a pedestrian and said the words, "Hey, you think you own the sidewalk?"

• • •

A tractor has passed you … and it was being pushed.

• • •

You've ever used a stoplight to get in a short nap.

• • •

You've ever made more than three U-turns within a block of your house to get something you forgot.

• • •

You've crossed two state lines with your left turn signal still on.

• • •

You've ever tried to report a fire truck for tailgating you.

• • •

Bumper Stickers for Seniors

I snore, therefore deal with it.

• • •

If you can read this, thank your bifocals!

• • •

Allow me to repeat myself.
Also, allow me to repeat myself.

• • •

I brake for leg cramps.

• • •

Honk if you still have all your
original body parts.

• • •

This car is a collectible—it collects dirt in the
carburetor, nails in the tires,
dents in the fender …

• • •

Honk if my driving annoys you.
Then I'll know I've done my job!

. . .

Flying

It's easy to tell the difference between flying
first class and flying coach. For one thing, first
class is usually *inside* the plane.

. . .

In first class, customers get complimentary
pillows. Budget customers are told to fluff up
their dinner roll.

. . .

It's so crowded in coach, that every time you
cross your legs, you end up with an extra one.

. . .

I always fly coach. It gives me a chance to get
reacquainted with my knees.

. . .

But flying scares me these days. I don't know about you, but I don't like it when airplanes have more loose parts than I do.

• • •

Did you hear they've raised the retirement age for pilots and flight attendants? I'm not saying how old my last stewardess was, but after she demonstrated the oxygen mask, she left it on.

• • •

I don't get air travel these days. No nail clippers, hedge trimmers, chain saws, or explosives are allowed aboard the aircraft. And then they give you a bag of pretzels you can't open without them.

• • •

And did you hear about that airplane that overshot the runway and ended up sliding into a gas station across from Burbank Airport? I guess the pilot didn't want to wait in line for the airport restrooms.

• • •

Airports are getting so crowded, airplanes are having to tuck in their wings just to land.

• • •

Don't you love how the pilot tells you to look out your window while he points out things you're flying over … like the Grand Canyon, the Rio Grande, your luggage … ?

• • •

Have you heard some airlines have been experimenting with pre-matching seatmates for a more enjoyable flight? I'm not sure what kind of questions are on the seat-match form, but here are a few I'd like to suggest:

1. Have you suffered any recent relationship problem, and do you consider the three-hour flight hardly enough time to cover all the issues?

2. Do you prefer the window seat, and if so, how many times have you been known to get up during a six-hour flight?

3. Do you drool, snore, or mumble in your sleep, and if so, are you opposed to being awaken by a whack on the side of your head with the in-flight magazine?

4. Do you typically carry your own lunch of boiled eggs and sardines when you fly?

5. Have you taken a bath within the current decade in which we are living?

6. Have you recently taken a vow of silence, and if so, how long is the waiting list to be your partner?

. . .

In-Flight Announcements You'd Rather Not Hear ...

"Please be careful when opening overhead compartments. We had to seat a few passengers up there, and we wouldn't want them falling out on you unnecessarily."

• • •

"The captain has turned on the 'Fasten Your Seatbelt' sign because we're coming up to some turbulence and our 'Hang onto Your Hat, Grandma' sign is against federal regulations."

• • •

"Sorry for the bumpy ride. The pilot was just dodging some trees."

• • •

"We're beginning our descent now ... hopefully on purpose."

• • •

"If you're worried about all the in-flight near misses airplanes have been having lately, we want to assure you that at our airline, it is our policy to never tailgate."

• • •

"We're next in line for takeoff. So as soon as we back up the aircraft, the rubber band will snap, and away we go!"

• • •

"Since this is a long flight, we recommend you do some sort of physical activity at regular intervals. Because of the glass windows, we do not recommend golf."

• • •

"If you're seated in an exit row and know you would push children and the elderly out of your way to save yourself, please notify your attendant. You will be reseated."

• • •

"If this is not your final destination, please stay on the plane while we try to figure out where in the world you're supposed to be."

• • •

"Please keep your seat belt fastened at all times. We have duct tape, and we're not afraid to use it."

• • •

"We'll be demonstrating the seat belt now. If you don't know how to operate one, we should probably tell you that Roosevelt isn't president anymore either."

• • •

"In the event of a water landing, please do not yell, "Cowabunga, baby!"

• • •

"In case of a water landing, your seat can be used as a floatation device. We do not, however, recommend using the wings as surfboards."

• • •

"In the event of a water landing, be assured that appropriate Beach Boy music will be played through the intercom."

• • •

"We'll be on the ground in fifteen minutes. Anyone needing to get off before that, talk to a flight attendant."

• • •

"We'll be on the ground in fifteen minutes … sooner if you all lean forward."

• • •

"Please return your seat to where it was before you reclined it that inch and a half."

• • •

"If you checked your carry-on luggage with the flight attendant—and provided you're not her size——your luggage will be waiting for you, planeside."

• • •

"If you'll look out the windows on the left side of the plane, you'll see the Grand Canyon. If it's on the right side of the plane, I'm not as good a pilot as I thought I was."

. . .

"For those of you who have never flown before … no, the wings do not flap when we take off."

. . .

"This is your pilot speaking. I'm back at the airport. You might wanna come back for me."

. . .

MARTHA'S COMEDY WRITING MEMORIES

Once fellow writer Gene Perret accompanied Bob Hope to the airport to pick up his wife, Dolores. As they watched Dolores step out onto the stairs of the private airplane, they noticed she was surrounded by several nuns who were traveling with her. Bob leaned over to Gene and said, "I don't know why she can't just buy regular flight insurance like everyone else."

• • •

Cruising

I'm not saying how seasick I get, but on my last cruise, they didn't assign me a cabin. They assigned me a railing.

• • •

My shower was so small, there wasn't room for me and the water at the same time.

• • •

Eating on a ship in a storm has its benefits. I mean, where else can you toss your salad after you eat it?

• • •

I'm not a big fan of cruising. If I want to spend that much time in the water, I just golf.

• • •

It was easy to tell I was on an inspirational cruise. My porthole had stained glass.

• • •

This isn't the first time I've had a room this size. I once got stuck in an elevator.

• • •

You Know You're at a Cheap Hotel When ...

There's such a big hole in the middle of the mattress, you can use the sheet as a trampoline.

• • •

MARTHA'S COMEDY WRITING MEMORIES

Being on Bob Hope's writing staff required a lot of fast writing. Like the time when Bob was scheduled to speak for a psychiatrists' convention. Needless to say, the jokes came fast and easy. The only problem was when Bob showed up at the venue, he discovered it wasn't a psychiatrists' convention. It was a chiropractors' convention! We had to quickly write all new material before he walked onto the stage.

• • •

Grumpy Old Men and Women on Vacation

At the Great Wall of China: "Chain link would have been cheaper."

· · ·

At Niagara Falls: "That constant dripping is going to keep me awake all night."

· · ·

At Big Ben: "So when does the cuckoo bird come out?"

· · ·

At the Grand Canyon: "And Florida thinks it has sinkholes!"

· · ·

More Senior Movies

Silence of the Hearing Aid Batteries

• • •

Dances with Bunions

• • •

Gone with the Wind—A Toupee's Journey

• • •

Star Wars (Senior Version):
The Foot Awakens

• • •

12 Angry Menopausal Women

• • •

A Streetcar Named "I Have No Idea Where
I'm Going"

• • •

The Sound of Snoring

• • •

Dial "M" for Medic

• • •

High Noon ... My Wake-Up Call

• • •

Remains of the Buffet

• • •

Ode to RVs

Driving Across America
Seeing All She Has to Give
My RV Rolls from State to State
'Cause I've Forgotten Where I Live

• • •

No One's Perfect

I live near a chemical waste dump...my stove.

• • •

For years my family thought mold was a frosting.

• • •

Rolaids—they're not just for breakfast anymore.

• • •

Dinner's done. Call 911!

• • •

The only person to ask for seconds of my cooking was the coroner at the inquest.

• • •

My dining room table has a garbage disposal.

• • •

When the meatloaf explodes, it's done.

• • •

At my house, the flies brown bag it.

• • •

"Honey, the fire department just called. They want to know if you'll be cooking tonight, or if they can take the night off?"

• • •

I've burned so many dinners, my self-cleaning oven surrendered.

• • •

My husband hates my cooking. He doesn't think meatloaf should have splinters.

• • •

At my house, the ants bring back the food.

• • •

I don't know if it means anything, but last night my trash compactor ate my kitchen.

• • •

I've found an easier way to serve leftovers.
I never clear the table.

. . .

Anyone who's been to my house knows you
can eat off my kitchen floors. There's usually
enough food there for three meals.

. . .

My house has seen more bugs than the F.B.I.

. . .

My roach motel is booked through August.

. . .

My house is so dirty … my vacuum has a
Weed Eater attachment.

. . .

My washing machine has a mildew cycle.

. . .

There's snow at the top of my dirty clothes pile.

. . .

I only clean the house when I can't find one of the kids.

. . .

I know it's time to change the bed sheets when the floral pattern takes root.

. . .

Our No-Pest strips have a control tower.

. . .

My house is so dirty that when the cockroach finally goes extinct, I know I'm going to get blamed.

. . .

I was such an ugly baby, my incubator had curtains.

. . .

Hey, Doc!

If doctors don't want us to live a sedentary lifestyle, why do they make us sit so long in their waiting rooms?

• • •

Doctors say our metabolism slows down as we age. Mine didn't just slow down. It pulled over and parked.

• • •

Doctors are becoming a lot more efficient. Nowadays, when you go in for a surgical procedure, they go ahead and remove your wallet at the same time.

• • •

My cataracts make it hard to tell the color green. Yeah, they didn't buy that in traffic court either.

• • •

I don't think the price of healthcare is too high. And I told them that, when I took out that loan for my Band-Aid.

• • •

Remember the good ol' days when the forms you had to fill out at a doctor's office had more to do with your symptoms than your credit rating?

• • •

Some doctors still make house calls. Yeah, they show up to repossess yours for their bill.

• • •

I finally got immunized against shingles. But I still get advertisements from roofers.

• • •

Research has shown that the most common procedure performed by doctors today is still the removal of the patient's wallet from his back pocket.

• • •

The price of prescription drugs is so outrageous, you need a sedative just to pay for your tranquilizers.

• • •

My blood is so tired. I have to wake it up to bleed.

• • •

I've been a diabetic for nearly fifty years. For me, that's well over forty thousand shots so far. But I look on the bright side. Now, I can take a drink and water all the houseplants at the same time.

• • •

You Know You've Joined a Cheap HMO When ...

Resetting a bone involves duct tape.

• • •

Their EKG machine bears a striking resemblance to an Etch-a-Sketch.

• • •

They get their Xrays developed at Walgreens.

• • •

You get a discount if you make up your own hospital bed.

• • •

Their thermometer goes up to 400 degrees and tastes a lot like turkey.

• • •

Their new surgical wing is a tiny house.

• • •

Their ambulance is listed as an Uber vehicle.

• • •

To visit their ER, you have to listen to a time-share sales pitch.

• • •

Their IV solution looks an awful lot like Kool-Aid.

• • •

Their mammogram machine doubles as the waffle iron in the hospital cafeteria.

• • •

In-Office Surgical Procedures

Sure, it's cheaper than a hospital, but if you happen to see any the of following, you might want to think twice about going through with the "in-office" procedure:

- The surgical tools have the Home Depot logo printed on them.

- Your doctor has to clear off his copy machine to make an operating table.

- The procedure room has a drive-thru.

- You notice the anesthesiologist is holding a hammer.

- Your oxygen mask says, "Property of American Airlines."

- You see the words, "For entertainment purposes only," on his medical license.

- Everyone in his waiting room is a malpractice attorney.

- His EKG machine also picks up talk radio.

- The defibrillator is a fork, and an electric outlet.

- He can't cut through the surgical supplies packaging.

• • •

Medical Definitions

Fibrillation: Not confessing to your doctor about the four chili dogs you had just before the chest pain began.

• • •

Anti-inflammatory: Not wanting to argue with your doctor over a billing error.

• • •

Bronchospasm: Leg cramps after a day of horseback riding with your grandchildren.

• • •

Atrophy: What you can win in the Senior Bowling League.

• • •

Carbohydrate: Drinking bottled water in your car.

• • •

Gastralgia: That nauseous feeling you get when looking at the price of gasoline.

• • •

Benign: A possible winning number in a game of Bingo.

• • •

Lower GI: A low-ranking member of the military.

• • •

CAT scan: Looking for the jazz station on your radio.

• • •

MARTHA'S COMEDY WRITING MEMORIES

I remember when my first comedy sketch got selected for one of Bob Hope's television specials. I was so excited, I could hardly stand it. The sketch took place in an elevator, and when I saw the crew bringing in the set for it, my heart skipped a beat. *No, I wasn't dreaming.* This was a major network, a Bob Hope television special, and my sketch!

However, as the taping continued throughout the day, my sketch kept getting pushed back in the schedule. Ultimately, it was moved back to after our dinner break.

When the other writers and I came back from Chadney's across the street from NBC, we walked into the studio and my heart sank to my stomach. The crew was tearing down the elevator set. "We're running long," the director explained. "We have to cut it."

My big moment was over before it ever even happened! Sure, I had jokes in the monologue, and bits and pieces here and there throughout the show, but this was a whole sketch that would have been mine.

But I didn't give up. A few years later, we did a show with a similar theme, and I resubmitted the sketch. I didn't really think it'd get picked twice, but sure enough, it did. This time, it made it into the show and starred Danny Thomas and Ann Jillian. So never say never. Yogi Berra was right, it really *isn't* over till it's over.

• • •

I'm shy. I'd talk to myself, but I don't want to be the first to say hello.

• • •

II

YOU GOTTA LAUGH

Men Versus Women

According to one survey, most men are happier than women by middle age. I think that's because men say what they feel and let the chips fall where they may, while women bury their feelings and eat the chips.

• • •

Woman Getting a Ticket

WOMAN: "But officer, other cars were passing you too, and they were going a lot faster than I was going. Why'd you pick on me?"

OFFICER: "Because you're the only one who waved as you went by."

• • •

Bob Hope on Golfing with Presidents

"I enjoyed golfing with President Kennedy, but he was always talking about Cuba. I finally told him, 'Hey, look, I can't help it where my golf ball lands.'"

• • •

"And John Kennedy didn't like the way I kept score. His philosophy was 'Ask not what your eraser can do for you …'"

• • •

"I didn't do much golfing with President Carter, which I regret. With all the water traps I've visited over the years, I could have used his naval experience."

• • •

"The incentive just wasn't there to golf with President Carter. It wasn't worth my time betting for peanuts."

• • •

"I always felt safe golfing with President Eisenhower. I knew if I took too long in the rough, he'd send a platoon in after me."

• • •

"But I think I've done more golfing with President Ford than any of the other presidents. Why not? My insurance is paid up."

• • •

"I would've golfed more often with President Ford, but we didn't have enough in common … like blood types."

• • •

"Jerry Ford's golf ball and my luggage have a lot in common. You know where they take off, but you're never quite sure where they're going to land."

• • •

"And I guess I'll never know what kind of a golfer George Washington was. He was always busy when I tried to set up a tee time."

• • •

"But I always love being invited to the White House. In fact, I'd go even if I wasn't mowing the lawn."

• • •

Sports

My age has really hurt my golf game. I just can't hunt and fish like I used to.

• • •

They call me Moses on the golf course. I know what it's like to wander around in the wilderness for forty years.

• • •

How's the Weather?

I'm not saying how much snow they got in Washington DC this week, but the Lincoln Memorial is now just a bust.

• • •

Washington had another blizzard come through. But it's okay. They're used to snow jobs.

• • •

It's been so cold in New York, the Statue of Liberty's carrying two torches now.

• • •

And can you believe all this rain? The streets are so flooded, you don't need brakes to stop your car. You need an anchor.

• • •

My swimming pool's overflowing ... which is pretty bad, considering before the storm, I didn't even have one.

• • •

And can you believe all the tornadoes that have been touching down lately? This is really unusual. Normally, we only see that much wind in an election year.

• • •

It's so hot, car thieves are only stealing convertibles.

• • •

Birthday Party Games
for the Over 50 Crowd

Pin the Tail on the Bald Spot: In this middle-aged version of the classic birthday party game, guests help the aging donkey look his best by taking hair from its tail and taping it into a comb-over.

• • •

Boomer Pinata: Think of all the frustration you can work out of your system with this party favorite. Mess with my social security? WHACK! Raise my heating costs? WHACK! Take away my senior discount? WHACK! WHACK! AND DOUBLE WHACK!

• • •

Spin the Ointment: Similar to Spin the Bottle, only instead of a kiss, the winner gets a neck massage with deep-heating rub.

• • •

Musical Recliners: This game is a lot like musical chairs, only the music is a lot slower, and between songs, you get to take a nap in the chairs.

. . .

Senior Scavenger Hunt: This senior version of an old favorite has all the players helping you look for all your misplaced personal items— glasses, car keys, cell phone …

. . .

Did You Know …

No matter how long you live, you will never use all the free condiment packets you've collected from fast food restaurants.

. . .

Some leggings just aren't worth the fight.

. . .

If you're serious about jogging, don't take your purse.

• • •

Some pants really do fit better when pulled up to your armpits.

• • •

After a certain age, magnifying mirrors should come with a warning.

• • •

Big journeys begin with a single step … or a broken GPS.

• • •

MARTHA'S COMEDY WRITING MEMORIES

One time when my mom attended a Bob Hope television taping, there was someone in the audience who not only laughed at Bob's jokes, but clapped as well. After every single joke. Bob seemed to appreciate it at first, but then, he started to get tickled. It got funnier when I found out that the clapper was my mom! After the show, I asked if she had enjoyed it. She said it was fun, and then she added, "But I didn't know which ones were your jokes, so I clapped at them all."

• • •

Menopause

Menopause just sort of sneaks up on you. One day you're thirty and your body temperature is normal. The next day you're fifty and people are gathering around you, using your body as a heating lamp.

• • •

Times Are A-Changing

Have you noticed how small cars are getting? I saw one the other day that looked like a golf cart had a baby. I'm not sure where the driver parked it, but my guess would be in his pocket.

• • •

In the News

Remember when authorities in Hawaii accidentally sent out an alert, warning the people that an incoming missile was on its way and they needed to take cover immediately? It took thirty-eight minutes to issue a correction. I think that's because they were all trying to figure out how to spell the word "oops."

• • •

And these oil spills are getting out of hand. The other day I saw a restaurant featuring high-octane halibut.

• • •

Did you hear about the fast food restaurant chain that got caught serving kangaroo meat in their burgers? It brings a whole new meaning to pocket sandwiches, doesn't it?

• • •

California and Earthquakes

And have you heard that California wants to divide and become three separate states now? I guess they got tired of waiting for the San Andreas Fault to do it for them.

• • •

With all the fires they get in California, wouldn't it just be easier to divide it into "smoking" and "non-smoking"?

• • •

California had another earthquake. I'm not complaining. It shook a few things into place at my house.

• • •

When it comes to earthquakes, most Californians won't even get out of bed unless it's at least a 6-pointer. Anything less than that, and they consider it a mandatory massage.

• • •

I don't mind earthquakes. I figure they're God's way of helping me get a hole in one.

• • •

My house is still up on a hill, but my view just got lowered.

• • •

I'm used to taking my car to work … not my waterbed.

• • •

And I've gotta tell you, it's a little unsettling to see my house passing me on the freeway.

• • •

They say the safest place to be when "The Big One" hits California is in a doorway … in Utah.

• • •

Possessions and Fashion

Money's getting tight for everyone. Last week a robber handed a bank teller a note that said, "This is a stick-up." She handed him one back that said, "This is an I.O.U."

• • •

Meddle not in the affairs of seniors, for you are on my lawn. I've got sprinklers and I'm not afraid to use them.

• • •

Can you believe how short skirts are getting these days? In my time, something that short wasn't called a skirt. It was called a belt.

• • •

MARTHA'S COMEDY WRITING MEMORIES

I came home one day and my son gave me a message that Bob Hope had called to say he was going to the doctor and needed jokes. I thought that was an unusual assignment, so before I turned in my doctor jokes, I thought I'd better call Bob and check. Bob laughed and said he was receiving an honorary *doctorate* from Gettysburg University and needed jokes.

• • •

Crime

I came from a tough town. Our orchestra had a siren section.

. . .

It's getting rough out there on our highways. These days, when someone honks at you, you can only hope it's because he loves Jesus.

. . .

All I can say is if you're going to tailgate someone these days, they'd better be towing you.

. . .

But I don't let road rage bother me. I just drive my tank in the slow lane and mind my own business.

. . .

Did you know Queen Elizabeth II uses her purse for sending secret signals to her staff? I don't know what all the signals mean, but here are a few she might not have thought of:

- If she is stuck with an overly talkative dinner guest, several raps of the purse to the side of the person's head should get the proper message across to her bodyguards.

- If an event has dragged on into the night, and she'd like it to come to an end, she could simply open up her purse and place it strategically over the royal crown.

- If the waiter has brought the check for her table, but she doesn't want to put everybody on her tab yet again, she can simply take her purse from her right arm and forthrightly sit upon it.

- And if she ever sets her purse down onto the floor with the strap wrapped around her leg, that's a clear signal that the stock market has dropped again. If she kicks it across the room, a crash is imminent.

• • •

Tax Cuts

Well, they finally cut our taxes. Isn't it nice to know the hand in your pocket is now your own?

• • •

Tax Hikes

They raised taxes, and the rich are feeling it. I hear Rodeo Drive just put in a tollbooth.

• • •

Martha's Comedy Writing Memories

For a comedy writer, there's nothing like hearing a legendary comedian saying one of your lines. That's why I was so excited to get to write an intro for Garth Brooks when he was the guest star on a Bob Hope special. The introduction started out, "And now, the most sought after performer in show business today …" But Bob kept getting tongue tied on the words and would say, "And now the most sawed-off performer in show business today." Repeated takes just kept getting funnier and funnier. Oh, well, it made it to the blooper shows.

• • •

Romance, Love, and Marriage

Marriage is hard work. If you think your marriage is perfect, you're probably still at your reception.

• • •

I'd go to the end of the world for my husband. Of course, if he'd just stop and ask directions, I wouldn't have to.

• • •

My husband and I call each other at least five times a day. It's not as romantic as it sounds. He calls me so I can find my phone, and I call him so he can find his.

• • •

My husband always encouraged me to pursue a writing career. At least I think that's what he meant every time he'd show me the door and say, "Don't forget to write."

• • •

I'd watch football with my husband, but he never wants to take the time to tell me who's pitching.

• • •

Among Hollywood celebrities, a marriage is considered a success if it makes it through the commercial.

• • •

A wife should never keep score of how many times her husband's wrong. That's what her mother is for.

• • •

The way some couples fight, you'd think the marriage vows said, "For griping and complaining, in nagging and harassing, as long as we both can duck."

• • •

Comedy Great Bob Hope

When my son was in junior high, he had to write a paper on a famous person. He chose Bob Hope. After doing the research, he asked me if I thought Bob Hope would agree to an interview. I didn't want to disappoint my son. After all, Bob Hope was … well, Bob Hope. I was certain he was far too busy for a junior high school report. So I told my son to call the office and ask the secretary, confident she would handle his request gently and tactfully. To all of our surprise, Bob took the call. He let my son interview him for fifteen to twenty minutes for a junior high school report! Bob Hope loved an audience … no matter what the age.

Another day, when I dropped off material at Bob's house, his dog, Snowjob, bit me on the foot. Bob felt terrible and sent me a telegram that said, "Dear Martha, please come back soon. I'm ready for another hors d'oeuvre. Love, Snowjob."

stars. I watched him joke with presidents and international dignitaries. But what intrigued me the most was his gratitude for his own good fortune … he did not take it for granted. His passion for show business, for life, and for laughter was unshakeable.

One afternoon, as I was again delivering some material to his home, Bob eagerly gave me a tour of his newly remodeled office. Dolores (his wife of 69 years) had done a beautiful job redesigning the room, and Bob wanted to show it off. He pointed out the various pictures hanging on each wall and down the hallway. There were numerous photos of him with celebrities—one with four living presidents, one with the late John F. Kennedy. As I viewed them, I noticed something interesting. It was almost as if he was on the outside looking in … as though he himself couldn't believe where his career had taken him and what an amazing, full life he had.

After describing the final photo, he paused. Glancing back at the gallery of memories, and with genuine awe and appreciation for all of them, he flashed that famous Bob Hope grin and said, "It's something, isn't it, Martha? It really is something."

• • •

Martha's Comedy Writing Memories

One day, Bob Hope's secretary had to call a hotel to book a room for him. When the hotel operator answered, the secretary explained that she was needing to book a room for Bob Hope. The clerk wasn't buying it, and said, "Look, I don't have time for these jokes." Bob's secretary said, "I'm serious. I'm calling for Bob Hope and he'd like a room for tonight." The skeptical clerk scoffed and started to hang up when the secretary jumped in and said, "Look, do you want me to put him on the line?" "Yeah, why don't you do that?" the clerk said sarcastically. After putting the clerk on hold, she explained the situation to Bob. Bob got on the line, and sang, "Thanks for the memory…" The clerk responded, "You're going to have to do better than that," and hung up on him!

• • •

Watching the Grandchildren

You know you're getting old when your grandchild asks you to close your eyes so he can give you a surprise … and you don't wake up until the following afternoon.

• • •

My six-year-old grandson asked his mother if he could have a donut. She told him, "No, you just had one." Without missing a beat, he said, "That was a different guy."

• • •

Grandchildren are God's way of saying you've taken enough naps.

• • •

Remember how God confused the languages at the Tower of Babel? Do you ever wonder if he's done the same thing to your teenage grandchildren?

• • •

One night, while on the phone with my granddaughter in another state, I told her that I would be flying out to see her soon. She said, "Come now!" I assured her it would be soon. "But I want you to come now!" she begged. This back and forth continued until I made her a deal. I told her I would see if there was a flight still leaving that night, and if there were any seats, Grandpa and I would come. I knew there weren't any more flights out that night, but I planned to keep my promise and check. She wasn't buying it. She said, "No. You go to Never Neverland, and then you can fly here *now*!"

• • •

Once while in the car with my three-year-old granddaughter, she suddenly yelled, "Get out of my face! Get out of my face!" For the life of us, her mother and I could not figure out who she was talking to as she was alone in the back seat. So we asked her if she was talking to one of us. "No," she said. "I'm talking to the sun!"

• • •

MARTHA'S COMEDY WRITING MEMORIES

I came home one night and there was a message on my answering machine from Bob Hope that said, "Hello, Martha. I tried calling Gene, and he's out speaking somewhere. I called Bob Mills, and he's out on the golf course. I called Si and Freddie, but they're not in, and you're probably out shopping. Didn't I used to have a career?"

• • •

A Joke's Journey

When I was a young child, I used to collect jokes. I love to laugh, so whenever I heard a funny joke, or read one in some magazine, I would write it down on a 3x5 card and add it to my collection of laughs. To this day, I still have that collection of jokes.

I was nine when I decided to try my own hand at humor writing. I wrote a "book" and titled it *No Fun Being Young*. It was about being the youngest of five, and at fourteen, I entered a newspaper cartoon gag-writing contest. To my surprise, my line was selected to be published.

Today, when I look back over decades of comedy writing, I'm amazed at how many dozens of notebooks, file cabinets, and hard drives I've filled up with my original jokes, not including all the receipts, church bulletins, napkins, and upholstery I have used for lack of paper.

Bob Hope stored all his jokes in a walk-in fireproof vault in his office adjacent to his Toluca Lake home. The jokes resided there during Bob's life in twelve, four-drawer file cabinets, organized by topic. His collection is now on file at the Bob Hope exhibit at the Library of Congress in Washington DC … some half million of them (528,000 jokes, to be more exact, or 85,000 pages of material). That's a lot of jokes, but then again, Bob did live to be 100.

This wealth of material is also a history lesson, because Bob lived in every decade of the last century. He saw it all and joked about it all. He entertained eleven US presidents, or as he once quipped, "I performed for eleven presidents … and entertained six." Bob's jokes have been digitally scanned, indexed by topic, and are available at the touch of a kiosk screen.

• • •

Phyllis Diller kept her jokes on 3x5 cards in a joke file cabinet, which consisted of 48 small file drawers. The collection has over 52,000 jokes and is now at the Smithsonian in the National Museum of American History. Like Bob's, Phyllis Diller's jokes are also divided by subject—cooking, marriage, housework, aging, and so on.

• • •

Joan Rivers left behind some 90,000 jokes. Milton Berle put 10,000 of his best jokes into a book, *Milton Berle's Private Joke File.*

• • •

It's nice to know that all these jokes have found a final resting place and are still on their mission to make people laugh.

One of a comedian's most cherished possessions is their collection of jokes. It's the same for a comedy writer. My jokes are on typing paper, about eight or ten to a page, and are kept in dozens of three-ring binders in my office. Or in scrapbooks. Or, as I mentioned earlier, I also find them scribbled on all sorts of things that over the years, I've repurposed as paper.

These thousands of jokes represent years of into-the-night writing sessions, and like Bob Hope, my collection is also a journey through history—at least the part of it I've lived. Sadly, too many great comedians are no longer with us, but their material can still be found on YouTube, CDs, books, and museums. And they're still making us laugh.

• • •

By the time you take the meanness, the agenda, and the profanity out of some of today's comedy, all you have left is the period.

• • •

Bob Hope's Cue Cards

Bob's cue cards have a lot of history. The reason Bob used them in the first place wasn't because he couldn't memorize the lines … the man had an incredible memory. Once he asked for a joke that he had performed at an event years before so he could use it again. He wanted to make sure he had it right. I looked through my files, and sure enough, there it was exactly on the date he remembered, and he knew it word for word.

The main reason he used cue cards was because of the respect he had for each joke. He wanted the delivery to be perfect … not too many words, not too few. And it had to be funny. Since his material was always relevant, we would often be writing jokes up to the last minute. Bob would call us for new jokes on whatever had just happened in the national news, or the local news where he would be appearing. As soon as he hung up the phone, he'd immediately walk onstage and do them from memory. So the cards weren't used to prompt his memory.

However, these cue cards did save Bob's life once. This story was recounted many times by Bob Hope himself, and it was included in the proclamation for Bob's 100th birthday celebration, as part of the Congressional Record. The incident happened during the Vietnam years, when Bob had to wait at the airport for his longtime cue card man, Barney McNulty, to unload 5,000 pounds of cue cards off the plane. Bob's arrival at the Saigon Hotel was then delayed, causing him to narrowly miss an enemy bomb that had been timed to detonate upon Bob's arrival.

Another memorable cue card story happened one year on our anniversary. My husband wanted to surprise me with a unique anniversary gift, so after a Bob Hope show taping, he went to Barney privately and asked him for an "anniversary favor." Barney graciously agreed, so the two of them sorted through the enormous stack of monologue cards for the night and found one that my husband knew for sure I had written. He then took the cue card around to the other writers and had them inscribe an anniversary greeting on it. He even caught up with Bob Hope in his dressing room and asked him to sign it.

Needless to say, I was both surprised and thrilled with the gift. Bob's inscription was: "Catch up to us!" Bob and Dolores were married for 69 years, which was quite the challenge. We're now closing in on fifty, so we're right on their heels.

This very special cue card is framed and has since hung in my home office in every house we've lived. It's a cherished memory from my comedy life, and it's always a source of interest to those who see it. Has it saved my life yet? Well, maybe not. But I can't tell you how many times laughter certainly has.

• • •

Martha's Comedy Writing Memories

Whenever it was time to write the script for another Bob Hope television special for NBC, the writers would gather together with Bob and decide what the theme of the show would be. We'd then turn in ideas for the various comedy sketches.

At one meeting, I turned in my ideas, but hadn't yet come up with a good enough ending for one of my sketches. So, I just wrote down a throwaway ending, figuring I'd come up with a better one later if the idea even got picked.

Bob sat at the end of the table and started thumbing through the pages of material all of us had turned in. He then stopped at that one particular sketch idea of mine, and said, "Martha's got a funny idea here," and he proceeded to read it to the group.

All went well until he got to my less than stellar ending. He stopped, looked up from the page, and said, "And then, Martha went to lunch."

• • •

Comedian Phyllis Diller

With her wild hair and out of this world fashion sense, Phyllis Diller was still one classy lady. She joked about her cooking (even though she was a great cook), joked about her housekeeping (even though her home was immaculate and beautifully decorated), and joked about aging (while getting more beautiful with each passing year, thanks to her cosmetic surgeries she often wisecracked about). Moreover, Phyllis Diller was not only the Queen of Comedy, she was also the Queen of Class.

Many of the comics of her generation had that kind of class. Among them, Danny Thomas, who fulfilled a promise he had made to St. Jude to open a children's hospital; Bob Hope, who tirelessly entertained our troops abroad; George Burns, who along with Bob Hope, donated millions to the Motion Picture Hospital and countless other charities. They all had it—class.

That generation of comedians had class when it came to their material too. They respected their audiences, never talked down to them, and never turned on them if a joke didn't work. They stayed away from material that might make their audience squirm.

They never forgot those who helped them on the way up the professional ladder either. Phyllis Diller would often credit Bob Hope for boosting her career. She was in her late thirties before she even began doing stand-up, and one night while performing in a Washington, D.C. club, Bob Hope slipped in and caught her act. She thought that she had bombed, but Bob caught up with her after the show and told her she was star material. His encouragement meant so much to her that she kept a rather large portrait of Bob Hope on prominent display in her home. She never forgot what his words meant to her that night, no matter how successful she became.

And talk about selling a line—no one could do it better than Phyllis Diller. It didn't matter what show or movie she was cast in, she brought 100 percent to her performances. Phyllis was a walking party. When she stepped into a room, you'd better hang on because she was ready to laugh. What a laugh she had … contagious and outrageous. You could hear Phyllis Diller's unmistakable laugh across a room, a restaurant, a studio, even around the world. It was easy to identify. To enjoy life with such abandon—that, too, was classy.

Phyllis was a great encourager as well. I would send her pages of jokes. She would often handwrite notes, indicating the ones she especially liked by commenting, "brilliant" or "dynamite." At times, she would make suggestions on how to improve a punchline. That kind of encouragement to a beginning comedy writer was even better than the check.

Phyllis not only blazed the trail for future female comedians, but she also helped bring many alongside her. She was unselfish in her support of future competition.

Phyllis Diller was a one-of-a-kind comedian who elicited laughter by simply walking onto the stage in her zany costumes. She was also a classical pianist, as well as a talented artist of whimsical paintings.

Phyllis had a childlike joy inside of her. She once told me that whenever she appeared on the Bob Hope TV specials, the two of them were like two kids playing in a sandbox of words. They both loved to dress up in outrageous costumes for their shows, and neither one ever lost that sense of wonder and fun.

To say Phyllis Diller left the world a better place than she found it would be an understatement. They say she died with a smile on her face. I'm not surprised. It was a fitting farewell from a funny lady who savored all that life had to offer, and shared so much joy with all of us … with a ton of class.

• • •

Slow Down

I'm not saying how many fast food restaurants I eat at, but the other day I caught myself ordering into my mailbox and then driving around my house.

. . .

Body Language Explained

Scratching Nose

Expert's Reason: Doubt, lying, feelings of rejection

Most Likely Reason:
Itching

Licking Lips

Expert's Reason: Flirtatious

Most likely reason: Getting that last taste of Ben & Jerry's

Frozen Broad Smile

Expert's Reason: Manipulative

Most Likely Reason: Forgot to remove whitening tray from mouth

OPEN JAW YAWN

Expert's Reason: Disinterested

Most Likely Reason: TMJ got stuck again

BLANK EXPRESSION

Expert's Reason: Not tracking conversation

Most Likely Reason: Starbucks is closed

FIDGETING

Expert's Reason: Nervous, suspicious

Most Likely Reason: Ticks

• • •

MARTHA'S COMEDY WRITING MEMORIES

Years ago, my husband and I were asked if we could pick up Ray Bradbury and drive him to a writers' event where he was to be the keynote speaker. Mr. Bradbury, a gifted science fiction writer, didn't drive or fly in airplanes. The more I thought about it though, the more I realized that we couldn't pick up someone as famous as Ray Bradbury in our old car. Thankfully, a friend, and the owner of a beautiful new Cadillac, came to my rescue by offering to switch cars with us for the evening. I was thrilled. I thoroughly enjoyed getting to discuss writing with Ray Bradbury, and everything was going along fine ... until it started to rain. My husband couldn't find the button that operated the defrost. During his multiple attempts, he ended up turning on the radio, the tape player, the air conditioner, the heater, and he even opened the sunroof! Ray Bradbury must have wondered what was going on, especially when we stopped for gas and couldn't find the gas tank. I eventually published a piece about the incident and sent it to Ray Bradbury. In my article I confessed how we had borrowed the car to impress him. Ray wrote me back and he couldn't have been more gracious. Yes, the Cadillac was nice, and I appreciated our friends letting us borrow it. But I'm sure Ray Bradbury would have been just fine with our old car.

• • •

I tried using body language.
I had nothing to say.

• • •

III

HANG ON—THE BEST IS YET TO COME!

Did You Know?

George Beverly Shea won a Grammy at 102.

• • •

Former President George Bush skydived on his 80th birthday.

• • •

Bob Hope got a hole-in-one on the golf course at 90.

• • •

Ray Kroc was 52 when he started the McDonald's franchise with his brothers.

• • •

Laura Ingalls Wilder published *Little House on the Prairie*, her first book, at 64.

• • •

Roget wrote the famous *Roget's Thesaurus* at age 73. He didn't consider himself old, though. Perhaps elderly, mature, getting on, antiquated, aged, advanced in years …

• • •

Grandma Moses never would have even started painting had it not been for her arthritis putting an end to her embroidering when she was 76 years old. Painting every day, she created well over a thousand works of art, twenty-five of those painted after her 100th birthday. Her last painting came to life as she was ending hers, at 101 years of age. The cause of death, according to her doctor? "She just wore out."

• • •

It's Not Over Till It's Over

Mark Twain's death was inaccurately reported while he was very much alive. Twain had gone to London on a speaking tour in 1897. In his absence, rumors began to spread that the humorist was seriously ill, and then, had ultimately died. When contacted by a reporter to clear up the matter, Twain informed him that the rumors of his death had been an exaggeration.

This same thing happened to Bob Hope—twice. In 1998, five years before his actual death, Bob's obituary not only ran on the website of the Associated Press, but it was announced on the floor of the United States House of Representatives, which was being broadcast live on C-Span. Bob was pleased with all the attention that his death was receiving, but quite surprised to hear of his passing when he otherwise felt pretty good.

Then, in 2003, just three months before his actual passing, a rough draft of his obituary was discovered on the CNN website, claiming that Bob Hope had died in 2000. Other notables had their obituaries prematurely posted as well in what became known as the "CNN Incident." The tributes, which had been pre-written, included announcements of the deaths of Bob Hope, Dick Cheney, Gerald Ford, Ronald Reagan, Fidel Castro, and Pope John Paul II.

The drafts had used the Queen Mother's tribute as a template, and some of the lines got mixed up with others. Both Bob and Dick Cheney were described as the "UK's favorite grandmother." Fidel Castro's obituary included part of Ronald Reagan's tribute, hence describing Castro as "lifeguard, athlete, movie star." Pope John Paul II was described as someone who "loved racing."

Once discovered, the tributes, which were housed in the development area of the CNN website and available to the public without a password, were immediately removed. Others who have had their death prematurely announced include: John Madden, Joe

Montana, *Leave It to Beaver*'s Jerry Mathers, Willie Nelson, William "The Refrigerator" Perry, Russell Crowe, and Macaulay Culkin.

The moral of all this? If you hear about your death, check your pulse before letting anyone measure you for funeral clothes. You might be pleasantly surprised.

• • •

Longevity of Comics

A quick read through of the following list, and you could get the impression that living life with a healthy, well-honed sense of humor sure has its benefits! I think there's something healthy about a good sense of humor …

Bob Hope—100

George Burns—100

Red Skelton—84

Phyllis Diller—95

Milton Berle—93

Bill Dana—92

Don Rickles—90

Joan Rivers—81

Moms Mabley—81

Jack Carter—93

Redd Foxx—68

Lucille Ball—77

Danny Thoma—79

David Brenner—78

Jackie Gleason—71

Red Buttons—87

Jonathan Winters—87

• • •

Attitude Changers

Opinions are like elbows. Everybody's got 'em, but they only bend one way.

• • •

Scripturally Sound

Which version of the Bible do most biblical scholars believe to be the most accurate? Large print.

• • •

The Senior Soapbox

Why aren't more companies targeting our age group? Why are we being ignored? Don't these companies realize they are missing a huge market? Granted, a visit to the local mall will prove that a lot of teenagers hang out there these days. But are they *shopping?* Are they *spending money?* No. They're "hanging." Contrary to what our skin might be doing, we members of the over-fifty crowd don't "hang." We shop, and not just window shop either. We're serious buyers. We pick up an item, check the price, and carry it right on over to the checkout counter and pay for it. Why? Because we only pick up what we're committed to buying … we need to conserve our energy.

• • •

The Advantages to Hiring Seniors

We won't leave skateboard marks on the walls of the building.

• • •

We won't call in sick because our new tattoo is infected.

• • •

You can send us to Milwaukee for a training conference, and we can find it on the map.

• • •

We're old enough to know that we don't know everything.

• • •

We'll show more respect for a boss thirty years our junior than some employees show to a boss thirty years their senior.

• • •

At staff meetings, we'll say "Yes, sir" or "Yes, ma'am," instead of "Yo, I'm down with that."

• • •

We won't use the company phone to call Australia just because we think the accent is cool.

• • •

We won't argue with you over whether or not we should remove our tongue ring, eyebrow ring, and various other body-piercing jewelry. Outside of the staples from our gall bladder surgery, we're not into having metal accessories puncturing our skin.

• • •

We would never say to a customer on the phone, "I woke up from my nap for this?"

• • •

We don't spend half as much time checking our blood pressure as the younger generation spends on social media.

• • •

MarTHa's coMeDy WriTinG MeMories

Bob Hope packed a lot of life and laughter into his 100 years, and he shared it with the world. For those of us who had the pleasure of watching him up close, we know how driven he was. But it was all done with a sense of fun. He enjoyed his life and career, and he genuinely loved to laugh. He treated his writing staff with respect too. Another of his quotes is in a frame in my office (a gift from fellow Bob Hope writer Gene Perret). It says: "'Who needs writers? I don't need writers—unless I want to say something.' – Bob Hope"

• • •

Emailed Obituary

"With all the sadness and trauma going on in the world at the moment, it is worth reflecting on the death of a very important person, which almost went unnoticed last week. Larry LaPrise, the man who wrote "The Hokey Pokey," died peacefully at the age of 93. The most traumatic part for his family was getting him into the coffin. They put his left leg in, and then the trouble started …"

. . .

And the Beat Goes On ...

CLASSIC TUNES FOR BABY BOOMERS:

Hank Williams: "You're A-Fib Heart"

Glen Campbell: "By the Time I Get
                      My Teeth In"

Otis Redding: "Sitting at the Doctor's
                      All Day"

Paul Anka: "Put Ben-Gay on My
                      Shoulder"

The Supremes: "Where Did My Mind
                      Go?"

Elvis: "Blue Suede Orthotics"

Neil Sedaka: "Standing up Is Hard
                      to Do"

Marvin Gaye: "I Heard It through
                      My Beltone"

The Comets: "Nap around the Clock"

• • •

Advantages to Aging

Strangers hold restaurant doors open for you, which usually puts you ahead of them in line.

• • •

Three sit-ups count as exercise.

• • •

You can walk down the street talking to yourself, and people assume you're on a headset.

• • •

You can fall asleep during a long, boring lecture and people assume you're mulling over the important points.

• • •

You can still wear pants that have shrunk, and no one asks if you're expecting a flood.

• • •

Ride on shopping carts.

• • •

You can say whatever you want as long as you're mumbling under your breath, and no one cares.

• • •

You get fewer offers for 30-year loans.

• • •

You can drive on the shoulder of the highway and you don't get a ticket.

• • •

Lights out by 8 p.m. saves a fortune in utility bills.

• • •

Senior Techy Terms

Download: What you do to get into your recliner.

• • •

Upload: What you do to get out of your recliner.

• • •

Hidden file: When you can't remember what name you gave it or where you filed it.

• • •

Clean sweep: What you do when the grandchildren get picked up after a day of babysitting.

• • •

The dark web: What you find when you're cleaning out your basement.

• • •

Virus: Why you need to use hand sanitizer on public computers.

. . .

Default: The setting you wish your body had, to return you to your original condition.

. . .

User: Scammers and con artists.

. . .

Internet: What fish never do when you're deep-sea fishing.

. . .

Memory: What you and your computer both seem to be running out of.

. . .

Update: What your Nehru jacket and platform shoes need to do.

. . .

Twitter: Your heart during an A-fib episode.

• • •

Shutdown: What your body does every night after eight o'clock.

• • •

Computer Signs for Seniors

}}}: -]
"Drat! My forehead fell in my eyes again."

• • •

: B – (
"Is it just me or are the bags under my eyes
getting worse?"

• • •

: - O
"I just had Botox. Can you tell?"

• • •

8 - /
"Has anyone seen my glasses?
Oh, silly me ... they're on my face."

• • •

S :)
"So, how do you like my new toupee?"

• • •

/ :)
"Can you tell I've got a comb-over?

• • •

{ }
"I don't recall these love handles being so prominent before."

• • •

: - x
"Who needs to count carbs when you've got duct tape?

• • •

Politics

The president says he wishes he didn't have to make all these important decisions. He wishes people wouldn't expect so much from him, and he wishes he didn't have to always have the right answer. In other words, he wishes he was vice president.

• • •

I can understand security being beefed up at the Super Bowl, but making the band march through a metal detector on the fifty-yard line at half-time is a bit much, don't you think?

• • •

More seniors should get into politics. We know how to trim the fat, live within a budget, and still think tweeting has something to do with bird watching.

• • •

I would never tweet in the middle of the night. The only thing that gets me out of bed at three o'clock in the morning is a leg cramp.

• • •

Ask not what your country can do for you, but how close the restrooms are located.

• • •

Remember when President Reagan got thrown from his horse? Nancy came up with a new slogan for him: "Just say whoa!"

• • •

Bob Hope on Washington

"I'd visit Washington more often, but Lincoln's got my chair."

. . .

"Actually, I do go to the White House a lot. I like to see how the commoners live."

. . .

"And can you believe all the mudslinging and accusations going on this election year? I haven't seen this many denials since my fan club was asked to identify themselves."

. . .

Bob Hope Introducing Then President George H. W. Bush at a Fundraising Dinner

"We were going to put Congress in charge of serving the dinner tonight, but we were afraid nothing would ever get passed."

• • •

Bob Hope on Diets

"Have you heard about the new Politician's Diet? You only eat your words."

• • •

"Phyllis Diller just lost 175 pounds. She couldn't catch her blind date."

• • •

Bob Hope on Air Travel

"Airlines are charging for baggage now. I can understand that … since my luggage usually ends up going to a lot more exotic places than I do."

• • •

"I hope they don't start charging us to use the overhead compartments. Where else would my writers sit?"

• • •

Bob Hope on Desert Storm

"Some of our troops are being sent back into the region. …Just when they'd finally gotten all the sand out of their boots too."

• • •

Bob Hope on California Earthquakes

"The governor visited six different California communities this past week. Then his house finally came to a stop."

• • •

"But I'm not worried about another disaster. Luckily, I've managed to stockpile plenty of water over the years. ... It's all in my golf shoes."

• • •

MARTHA'S COMEDY WRITING MEMORIES

Whatever was happening in the news, Bob Hope wanted to talk about it. So, when an earthquake happened one morning in California, my husband, who was an LAPD sergeant at the time, got a call to work the disaster. I got a call to write jokes about it for Bob Hope. My call made it through first.

• • •

Senior Definitions

Egomaniac: Someone who believes the best things in life are me.

. . .

Mother-in-law: The original heavy meddler.

. . .

Spring weeds: The floral majority.

. . .

Hypochondriac: A person of ill dispute.

. . .

Country music songwriter: Someone who keeps his prose to the rhinestone.

. . .

Bachelor: A man with no rings attached.

. . .

Beginning comedy writer: All smirk and no pay.

• • •

Procrastination: What one vows to give up some day.

• • •

Success: What you get when you put do and do together.

• • •

Broadway for Seniors

Annie, Get Your Girdle

• • •

Gramma Mia!

• • •

Hello, Doctor!

• • •

Hamilton … and Other Childhood Friends

• • •

After the Fall … and I Can't Get Up

• • •

I Love You, You're Perfect …
Now, What Was I Talking About?

• • •

Beauty and the Plastic Surgeon

• • •

I'm Miserables

• • •

West Side Bursitis

• • •

Owe RENT

• • •

Much Ado about Cholesterol

• • •

Phrases We Don't Hear Anymore

"I'll take a nickel's worth."

• • •

"Would you like me to check
under your hood?"

• • •

"Here's your change."

• • •

"Oh, boy, I just found a penny!"

• • •

"Free dinnerware with fill-up."

• • •

"I can't wait to get their new 8-track."

• • •

Facing Life with Laughter

What many comedians have learned throughout their lives is that "when life gets tough, the tough start laughing." They certainly didn't have easy lives. Most comedians don't. They've simply learned to use their divinely designed coping equipment to its maximum ability.

Bob Hope had a knack for letting stress go. Whenever something happened that upset him, he would either address it or leave it alone, and then let it go. He didn't seem to harbor it for very long, or allow it to fester.

Comedians, and those who appreciate or work in comedy, also have a skewed way of looking at circumstances. It's not denial—they know all too well that life is tough, and things don't turn out as expected or desired all of the time. Sometimes friends are there for you and sometimes they fail you; good health comes and goes; and troubles and bills are always present—they just appear under a different name. Comedians look for the funny in it all. They have their radar up to discover any way they can get a few laughs over a situation. Why? Because laughter puts problems in perspective.

These comedy geniuses learned that lesson. No one would pay money to hear a performer step up on the stage and spend the hour ruminating on his or her problems. An audience wants to laugh with someone who has learned to roll with the punches, look beyond circumstances, and find the humor.

Genetics plays a part—exercise and eating healthy does as well. But don't overlook the importance of a positive attitude and a well-nourished sense of humor in your life plan. In other words, while taking your vitamins, don't forget to take care of your funny bone too!

• • •

MARTHA'S COMEDY WRITING MEMORIES

Bob would often put the sketches together using chunks of material from each of us. The danger to this was sometimes mistakes happened. Like one sketch with Brooke Shields where the script had given her three entrances and no exits. No wonder Brooke was on so many Bob Hope specials—we never let her leave!

• • •

And Speaking of Exits, Bob Hope May Have Made the Best One ...

As Bob Hope neared the end of his life, his wife asked him where he wanted to be buried. He simply said, "Surprise me."

• • •

About the Author

Martha Bolton is an Emmy, Dove, and Writers' Guild Award nominee, and was a staff writer for Bob Hope for over a decade and for Phyllis Diller, Mark Lowry, and many other comedians. She is the playwright for Blue Gate Musicals, with seven plays that have been playing in Indiana, Ohio, and Pennsylvania. Two of those plays are based on her novels, *Josiah for President* and *The Home Game*. *The Home Game* was awarded a Golden Scroll Merit Award for Fiction. She is married to her high school sweetheart and is the mother of three and the "Nana" to nearly a baseball team of grandchildren.